MOMMA, WHO WAS IRENA SENDLER?

WRITTEN BY:
CATHY WERLING

ILLUSTRATED BY:
MAGGIE RAGUSE

PUBLISHED BY:

Lowell Milken Center
FOR *Unsung Heroes*

It was almost bedtime for Blair, and she had mixed feelings on this particular night. She loved cuddling up with her mom to read stories together before falling asleep. She also knew that falling asleep this night meant that she would soon be waking up on the day Mommy had to leave for her trip.

Blair's mom, Megan, and others she worked with would be flying to a faraway city to put on a play for a big group of people. Blair knew that the play was about a woman named Irena Sendler and that it was called, "Life in a Jar." However, she didn't really know a lot about the story of the woman named Irena.

She had never thought to ask her mom about the play because it was just part of Mommy's job. She knew that dads and moms went to work so that their families could have money for food and clothes and houses. Blair thought that was just the way it was.

Tonight, though, she wanted to know more. She wanted to make this special time last longer for the two of them because her mom would be leaving on the airplane the next day. As they snuggled side by side, Blair said, "Mommy, I don't want you to read a book tonight. Instead, I want you to tell me about what you do, and about the lady named Irena, and the jars."

Megan was a bit surprised at Blair's request. She had often wondered when she would have the chance to explain her work to Blair, and if Blair would understand. Megan wanted to share that her life's work was so much more than a job to her – it was her passion!

Her thoughts were interrupted by Blair's next question, "Mommy, please, I want to know. Why do you have to tell people about Irena's story?"

Megan realized it was time to tell her daughter about Irena Sendler. She needed Blair to understand why her life's work centered on telling others about Irena, as well as sharing little-known stories of other people who had become unsung heroes in the course of history.

Blair snuggled closer to her mom, as Megan began the story, "When I was 14 years old, I was working with some other girls on a history project in school. We were supposed to find a true story about an unsung hero, a person who was not well known, but who had done some important things to help people. It was when we started looking for such a hero that my friends and I found out about Irena Sendler – and her story."

"Irena lived in the country of Poland, far across the ocean from America. Her father was a doctor, and he taught Irena to always be willing to help people, no matter how hard it might be. In fact, he had helped many, many sick people because no other doctors would help them."

"After her father became ill and died, Irena knew that she wanted to be the kind of person he had been. She, too, wanted to do all she could for people who needed her help."

"Irena grew up to become a social worker, a person who helped people through hard times in their lives. She and other workers found ways to assist struggling families with food, money, jobs, or whatever they might need."

"During the time Irena was a social worker, a horrible war broke out in the world and in the country where she lived. Adolf Hitler, a very evil leader of a group called the Nazis, had decided that 'ruling the world' was his goal."

"The Nazis marched into the country of Poland and took control. There were groups of people that Hitler and his armies did not feel were 'good enough' to be part of the 'empire' he wanted to rule. One such group was the Jewish people, who had their own religion."

"Hitler sent his men into their homes to arrest them and put them in a section of the city surrounded by large walls. The Nazi soldiers were very cruel to these people, hurting them and even killing many of them."

"Irena Sendler was not Jewish, so she and others with whom she worked were allowed to stay in their own homes. However, they were not allowed to help the Jewish people in any way. If they were caught doing so, they would be punished in very bad ways."

"One of these walled-in areas was in Warsaw, Poland, Irena's city. She and others who worked in the social welfare department saw the awful things happening to the Jewish people. Irena kept remembering her father's words about doing all she could to help others, no matter how difficult."

"She and a group of her co-workers devised plans that would help them get into the 'ghetto,' that area where all of the Jews were being held captive. Because more than 400,000 Jews were crowded into this small area, life for them was horrible. Many were starving and catching terrible diseases. Irena hoped that she and her co-workers could figure out ways to get some of the Jewish people out to safe places."

"Irena knew that Hitler's Nazi soldiers did not want to be around people with a terrible disease called Typhus. They were afraid of catching this sickness from the Jewish people. Irena's idea was that she and her workers would be allowed to enter the ghetto if they were disguised as nurses taking supplies to those who were sick."

"Irena's plan worked, and they were allowed to go into the ghetto but were being watched very closely by the Nazi soldiers. When Irena was in the ghetto, she knew the Jewish people needed help quickly. Besides the many that were suffering and dying from sickness and starvation, there were many more that would soon be killed as part of Hitler's need to rid his 'empire' of any people he did not want."

"Because children were smaller and easier to hide, Irena began finding ways to get children and babies out to safety. Arrangements were made to find families, as well as orphanages and convents, that would take care of these Jewish children and give them safe homes."

"She and her workers devised secret plans to safely get the children out of the ghetto. They first found safe places for the orphans, children who had already lost their parents and had no family to watch out for them."

"The orphaned children were disguised in clothing that would not make them look like Jewish children. They were then given Polish names and taught to speak a Polish prayer or other simple Polish words. The children were then walked by the workers through secret exits or sent through underground tunnels that led them out of the ghetto. Other helpers were waiting to take them to safety."

"As the danger of death became more and more real for the Jewish families in the ghetto, Irena knew that she and the other rescuers must work even harder to help save those they could. She talked to the parents who feared that not only would they lose their own lives, but that their children would die, too."

"Irena offered them the hope to save the lives of their children. She and her co-workers gave safe medicine to the babies and very small children that would make them sleep. Then they would hide the sleeping children in their supply bags, cases, and other containers which they'd been allowed to bring into the ghetto. They could then walk out through the gates with the hidden children and take them to places of safety."

"It was so very hard for parents to give their sons and daughters to Irena because of their great love for them. Most importantly, it was that great love that moved them to want the best for their children, the chance for them to be safe and cared for."

"The parents began giving their children to Irena and the other rescuers. Irena promised the parents that her goal was to help make life the best it could be for the children. She also had a plan to make sure the children always knew about the Jewish families into which they had been born, hoping they would someday be back with those same families."

"After the children were delivered to their new, safe homes, Irena used small slips of paper on which she wrote the Jewish name of each child, as well as the new Polish family name and the location to which the child was taken. She then put the slips of paper in milk jars. When the jars were filled, she and her friend, Jaga, would bury the jars under an apple tree outside Jaga's home."

"Because people needed food and would not cut down any fruit trees for their firewood, Irena and Jaga believed the jars would be safe under the apple tree. Irena planned to dig up the jars after the war ended, find the Jewish children, and hopefully reconnect them to their Jewish families."

"Irena was able to help save many, many children during that awful war. Her own life was in constant danger, and she was even captured by the Nazis and hurt very badly. Her friends were able to help her escape from prison, but she had to go into hiding until the war was finally over. Hitler and his Nazi armies were defeated by many countries, including the United States, who knew his evil plan must be stopped."

"After the war, Irena and some of the other rescuers dug up the jars and began the search for the children. It is not known how many, but they did find a number of those children and were able to let them know about their wonderful Jewish families who had loved them so very much."

"Not long after that, another country took over Poland. The ruler of that country would not honor any brave Polish people like Irena. He did not want them to stand up against things they thought were wrong in his government. So, Irena's story was not known by many people, and her bravery in saving the children was hidden for many years."

As Megan finished the story and continued to snuggle with her daughter, she couldn't help but remember her last trip to Poland and another hug, the one she had received from an aging Irena. Irena's precious words had proven so true in Megan's life, "You cannot separate people based on race, religion, or creed, only by good and evil, and then good will triumph."

Megan's thoughts were interrupted as Blair hugged her even tighter, saying, "Now I know why you called Irena's story, 'Life in a Jar.' Each child who had a name in those jars was someone whose life was saved by Irena and the other rescuers. Mommy, you <u>do</u> need to tell her story. Irena was so brave, and she didn't help those people just so she could become a hero. She did it because they needed someone to help. It was the right thing to do! Now you are sharing her story because people should know how important it is to help others when they need us. It is the right thing to do."

Blair relaxed against her mom, her eyes ready to close.

With one last hug, she sleepily whispered, "I want to be a person

who does the right thing, too, Mommy … just like you … and Irena."

LIFE IN A JAR: THE IRENA SENDLER PROJECT

History Teacher, Norm Conard
1999

Irena Sendler
circa 1939

THE DISCOVERY

In the fall of 1999, Norm Conard, a high school teacher in Uniontown, Kansas, encouraged three students to work on a National History Day project which would reach outside the classroom to families in the community, contribute to history learning, teach respect and tolerance, and meet their classroom motto, "He who changes one person, changes the world entire."

Two 9th graders, Megan Stewart and Elizabeth Cambers, and an 11th grader, Sabrina Coons, accepted the challenge to enter a project in the National History Day program. They discovered a short clipping from a March 1994 issue of News and World Report, which said, "Irena Sendler saved nearly 2,500 children from the Warsaw Ghetto in 1942." Mr. Conard encouraged the girls to search for primary sources since he had not heard of this woman or her story. Through their research, the girls found that Irena's story was true, and more importantly, they discovered, in early 2000, that Irena Sendler was still alive and living in Poland, at the age of 90.

Megan Stewart 1999   Elizabeth Cambers 1999   Sabrina Coons 1999

THE LIFE IN A JAR PROJECT

The students wrote a performance entitled Life in a Jar, in which they portrayed the life of Irena Sendler. They performed for many groups throughout North America and in Europe. As of 2018, the play has been performed 380 times, with over 50 students involved in the project.
Learn more at **irenasendler.org**.

FROM KANSAS TO THE WORLD

On May 22, 2001, Mr. Conard traveled with the students and several family members to Warsaw, Poland. They spent time with Irena Sendler and met some of the members of the underground and adults who had been children saved by her. One such woman was Elzbieta Ficowska who shared her beautiful story of being rescued by Irena at the age of five months, carried out in a carpenter's box.

Irena's story, previously hidden for so many years, became international news and was finally reaching others. The students were called "rescuers of the rescuer's story" by one of the children Irena saved.

The three original students are now adults and married, with their own children. Megan (Stewart) Felt is the Program Director of the Lowell Milken Center for Unsung Heroes, Elizabeth (Cambers) Hutton is a history teacher in Missouri, and Sabrina (Coons) Murphy is an elementary teacher in Kansas.

Norm Conard, the history teacher, is currently the Executive Director of the Lowell Milken Center for Unsung Heroes in Fort Scott, Kansas.

Irena with the Students

THE LEGACY

Irena Sendler passed away on May 12, 2008, which, very meaningfully, happens to be Megan (Stewart) Felt's birthday. Irena was buried in a Warsaw, Poland cemetery.

Her family and many of the rescued children continue to tell her story of courage and valor. The Life in a Jar students carry on her legacy through the play, through school presentations and study guides, through the exhibit at the Lowell Milken Center for Unsung Heroes, and on the LMC website. Irena Sendler, who was unknown when the project started, is now known throughout Poland and the world.

Irena Sendler
in 2008,
at the age of 98

Blair, with her mommy, Megan

THE AUTHOR

Cathy Werling is an award-winning elementary educator living in Fort Scott, Kansas. Her passion for helping students develop positive character traits and seek out worthy role models led to her part time work at the Lowell Milken Center for Unsung Heroes. *Mommy, Who Was Irena Sendler?* is the third book in her series of children's books about these humble heroes. By sharing Irena's story with children, Cathy helps them understand the power of one person to make a positive difference in the world around them and inspires them to find that power within themselves.

THE ILLUSTRATOR

Maggie Raguse, owner of Raguse Creative Services in Portland, Oregon, has been a prolific illustrator and graphic designer for over three decades. She specializes in fashion illustration and surface design and has a warm place in her heart for illustrating children's books. Collaborating with Cathy Werling in supporting the mission of the Lowell Milken Center for Unsung Heroes has been a rich and rewarding experience for her.

CPSIA information can be obtained
at www.ICGtesting.com
Printed in the USA
BVHW020750121121
621449BV00002B/11